For exams in December 2015 and June 2016

ACCA Diploma in
International Financial Reportin

First Edition 2011, Fourth Edition 2015

ISBN 9781 4727 4025 0

Previous ISBN 9781 4727 2884 5

British Library Cataloguing-in-Publication Data

A catalogue record for this book is available from the British Library

Published by

BPP Learning Media Ltd,
BPP House, Aldine Place,
142-144 Uxbridge Road,
London W12 8AA

www.bpp.com/learningmedia

Printed in the United Kingdom by Ricoh

Ricoh House
Ullswater Crescent
Coulsdon
CR5 2HR

Your learning materials, published by BPP Learning Media Ltd, are printed on paper obtained from traceable sustainable sources.

Welcome to BPP Learning Media's **Passcards** for the Dip IFR.

- They **focus on your exam** and **save you time**.

- They incorporate **diagrams** to kick start your memory.

- They follow the overall **structure** of the BPP Learning Media Study Texts, but BPP Learning Media's Dip IFR **Passcards** are not just a condensed book. Each card has been separately designed for clear presentation. Topics are self contained and can be grasped visually.

- Dip IFR **Passcards** are still **just the right size** for pockets, briefcases and bags.

Run through the **Passcards** as often as you can during your final revision period. The day before the exam, try to go through the **Passcards** again! You will then be well on your way to passing your exams.

Good luck!

Contents

1: The IASB and the regulatory framework

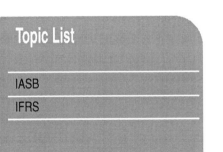

Topic List

IASB

IFRS

You should be aware of the structure of the IASB and the due process for producing IFRSs.

IASB

Financial reporting is governed on a worldwide basis by the International Accounting Standards Board. Decisions on accounting principles are made by the Board and issued in the form of IFRSs.

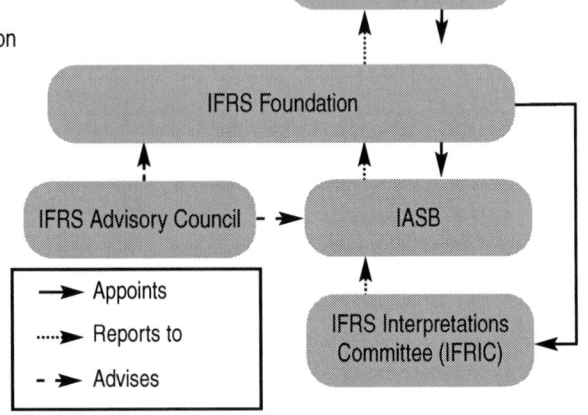

- → Appoints
- ·····▶ Reports to
- - ▶ Advises

The IASB issues and promotes the use of IFRSs. IFRSs are based on the IASB Conceptual Framework. The procedure for issuing an IFRS can be summarised as follows.

1. During the early stages of a project, IASB may establish an **Advisory Committee** to give advice on issues arising in the project. Consultation with the Advisory Committee and the IFRS Advisory Council occurs throughout the project.

2. IASB may develop and publish **Discussion Papers** for public comment.

3. Following the receipt and review of comments, IASB develops and publishes an **Exposure Draft** for public comment.

4. Following the receipt and review of comments, the IASB issues a final **International Financial Reporting Standard**.

Notes

2: Conceptual framework for financial reporting

Topic List

Conceptual framework

GAAP

Objectives: assumptions

Qualitative characteristics

Elements

Capital maintenance

The IASB's Conceptual Framework for Financial Reporting *represents the conceptual framework on which all IFRSs and IASs are based.*

Conceptual framework – a statement of generally accepted theoretical principles which form the frame of reference for financial reporting.

Advantages

- Avoids 'patchwork' or firefighting approach

- Less open to criticism or political/external pressure

- Some standards may conflict with one another

Disadvantages

- Financial statements are intended for a variety of users – single framework may not suit all

- May need different standards for different purposes

- Preparing and implementing standards is still difficult with a framework

GAAP signifies all the rules, from whatever source, which govern accounting.

Sources for individual countries

National company law

National accounting standards

Local stock exchange requirements

IASs/IFRSs if applicable

Non-mandatory sources

Other countries' statutory requirements

In many countries, like the UK, GAAP does not have any statutory or regulatory authority or definition. GAAP is a dynamic concept.

| Conceptual framework | GAAP | **Objectives: assumptions** | Qualitative characteristics | Elements | Capital maintenance |

Objectives of financial statements

Financial position

Statement of financial position

Financial performance

Statement of profit or loss and other comprehensive income

Statement of cash flows

Changes in financial performance

Statement of profit or loss and other comprehensive income

Statement of cash flows

Statement of changes in equity

Notes to the financial statements

Directors' report

Underlying assumption ➡ **Going concern**

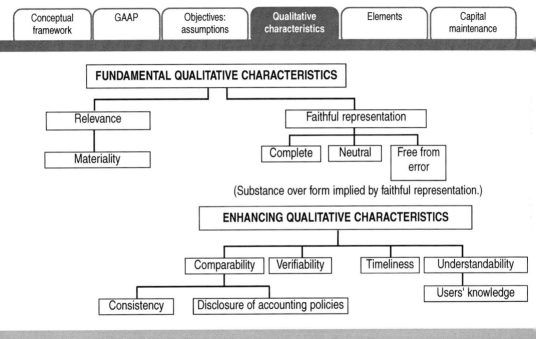

FUNDAMENTAL QUALITATIVE CHARACTERISTICS

Relevance

Materiality

Faithful representation

Complete | Neutral | Free from error

(Substance over form implied by faithful representation.)

ENHANCING QUALITATIVE CHARACTERISTICS

Comparability | Verifiability | Timeliness | Understandability

Consistency | Disclosure of accounting policies

Users' knowledge

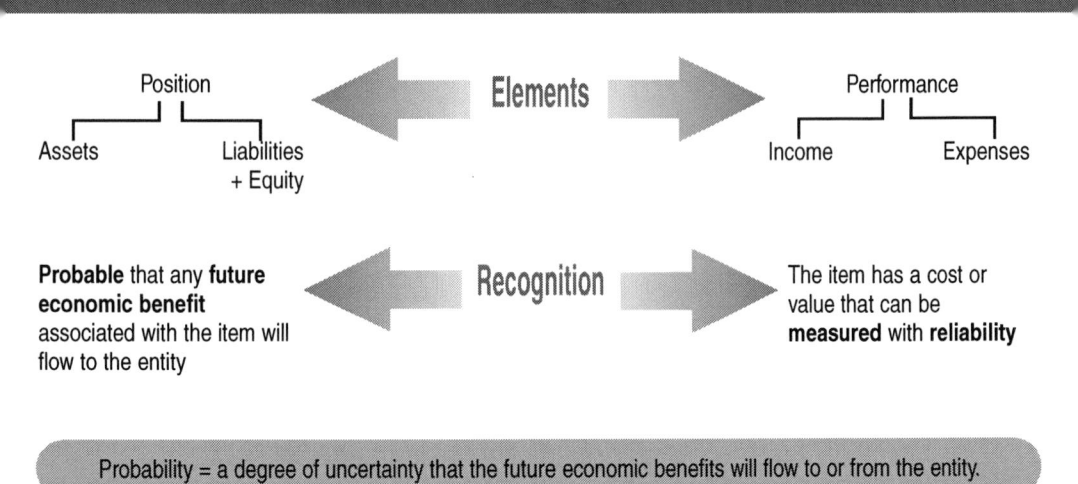

| Conceptual framework | GAAP | Objectives: assumptions | Qualitative characteristics | **Elements** | Capital maintenance |

Elements

Position
Assets — Liabilities + Equity

Performance
Income — Expenses

Recognition

Probable that any **future economic benefit** associated with the item will flow to the entity

The item has a cost or value that can be **measured** with **reliability**

Probability = a degree of uncertainty that the future economic benefits will flow to or from the entity.

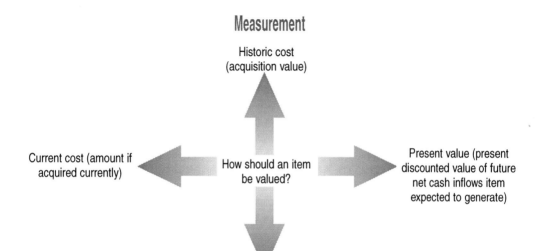

Measurement

Historic cost (acquisition value)

Current cost (amount if acquired currently)

How should an item be valued?

Present value (present discounted value of future net cash inflows item expected to generate)

Realisable (settlement) value (amount selling in current state)

2: Conceptual framework for financial reporting

Financial capital maintenance

Profit is earned if the financial amount of the net assets at the end of a period exceeds the financial amount of net assets at the beginning of a period after excluding any distributions to, and contributions from, owners during period.

Can be measured in either nominal monetary units or units of constant purchasing power.

Physical capital maintenance

Profit is earned if the physical productive capacity (or operating capacity) of the entity at the end of the period exceeds the physical productive capacity at the beginning of the period, after excluding any distributions to and contributions from, owners during the period. This concept requires the current cost basis of measurement.

The selection of the measurement bases and concept of capital maintenance together determine the accounting model used.

3: Revenue

Topic List

IFRS 15

5-Step model

Performance obligations

IFRS 15 *Renevue from contracts with customers* now replaces IAS 18 *Revenue* and IAS 11 *Construction contracts*.

IFRS 15 *Revenue from contracts with customers*

The core principle of IFRS 15 is that revenue is recognised to depict the transfer of goods or services to a customer.

Transfer of goods and services is based upon transfer of **control** over those goods and services.

A contract with a customer contains a promise to transfer goods or services.

This promise is defined in IFRS 15 as a **performance obligation**.

The 5-step model in IFRS 15 is:

Step 1: Identify the contract with the customer

Step 2: Identify the separate performance obligations

Step 3: Determine the transaction price

Step 4: Allocate the transaction price to the performance obligations

Step 5: Recognise revenue when (or as) a performance obligation is satisfied

A performance obligation can be satisfied **at a point in time** or **over time**.

Where a performance obligation is satisfied at a point in time, this will be the point in time at which **control is transferred to the customer**.

Indicators of this are:

- The entity has a right to payment
- The customer has legal title to the asset
- The customer has taken possession of the asset
- Risks and rewards have been transferred
- The customer has accepted the asset

Where a performance obligation is satisfied **over time** it is necessary to establish the amount of performance completed during the accounting period. This can be measured using **output methods** (such as surveys of work completed) or **input methods** (such as labour hours or costs incurred).

Contracts where performance obligations are satisfied over time are common in the construction industry.

Contract where performance obligations are satisfied over time

Outcome can be estimated reliably

An entity must determine what amounts to include as revenue and costs in each accounting period

Outcome cannot be estimated reliably

Recognise contract revenue and contract costs by reference to amount of performance obligation satisfied

Any expected loss should be recognised as an expense immediately

Recognise revenue only to extent of contract costs incurred that it is probable will be recovered. Recognise as expense in period incurred

Where the outcome of a contract can be estimated reliably, a proportion of contract revenue and costs should be recognised in profit or loss by reference to the stage of completion (ie a proportion that fairly reflects the amount of work done). This represents the amount of performance obligation satisfied.

The stage of completion can be calculated in various ways including:

Proportion of contract costs incurred:

$$\frac{\text{Costs to date}}{\text{Total estimated costs}} \times \text{Estimated total revenue/costs}$$

Input method

Surveys of work performed:

$$\frac{\text{Work certified}}{\text{Contract price}} \times \text{Estimated total revenue/costs}$$

Output method

Disclosure

Statement of profit or loss	
Revenue (x% × total contract revenue)	X
Expenses (x% × total contract cost)	(X)
	X
Expected loss	(X)
Recognised profit/loss	X

Statement of financial position	
Contract asset/liability	
Contract costs incurred	X
Recognised profits less recognised losses	X
	X
Less amounts invoiced to date	(X)
	X/(X)
Trade receivables	
Amounts invoiced to date	X
Less cash received	(X)
	X

Notes

4: Accounting for tangible non-current assets

Topic List

IAS 16
IAS 20
IAS 40
IAS 23

IAS 16 should be familiar to you from your earlier studies. IAS 20, on government grants, is a straightforward standard and you should have few problems with it.

Borrowing costs are covered by IAS 23 (revised).

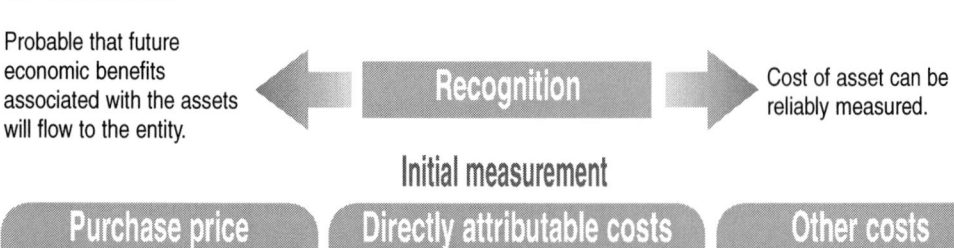

| IAS 16 | IAS 20 | IAS 40 | IAS 23 |

IAS 16 *Property, plant and equipment* covers all aspects of accounting for these items, which are most tangible non-current assets.

Probable that future economic benefits associated with the assets will flow to the entity.

Recognition

Cost of asset can be reliably measured.

Initial measurement

Purchase price

Import duties

Non-refundable purchase taxes

LESS

Trade discounts/rebates

Directly attributable costs

Site preparation

Delivery/handling

Testing

Professional fees

Other costs

Estimate of dismantling/removal costs and site restoration (IAS 37)

Finance costs (IAS 23)

Subsequent expenditure

Same criteria as initial costs. Otherwise do not capitalise but charge to profit or loss.

Subsequent measurement

Cost model	Revaluation model	Depreciation
■ Cost less accumulated depreciation and accumulated impairment losses	■ Revalued amount (fair value at the date of revaluation) less subsequent accumulated dep-reciation and impairment losses ■ Revalue sufficiently regularly so carrying amount not mater-ially different from fair value ■ All items of same class should be revalued	■ Systematic basis over useful life reflecting pattern of use of asset's economic benefits ■ Periodic review of useful life and depreciation method and any change accounted for as change in accounting estimate

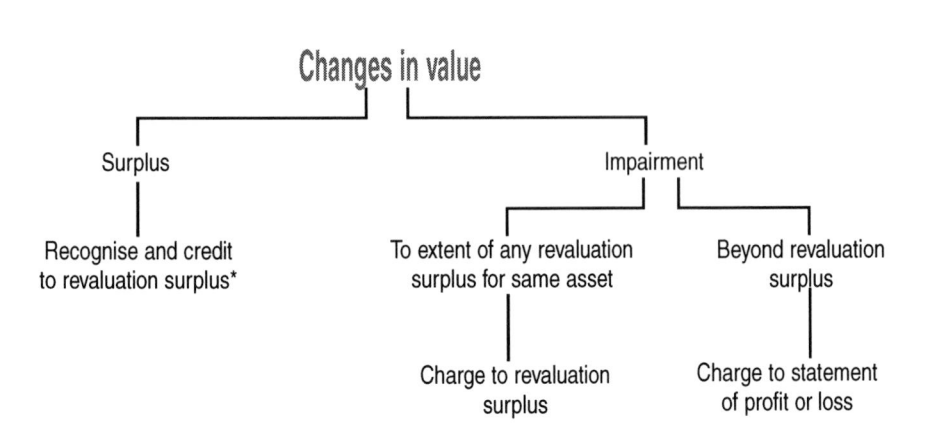

Changes in value

Surplus

Recognise and credit to revaluation surplus*

Impairment

To extent of any revaluation surplus for same asset

Charge to revaluation surplus

Beyond revaluation surplus

Charge to statement of profit or loss

* Unless reversing a previously recognised revaluation decrease of the same asset, in which case recognise as income to the extent of reversal of the previous decrease.

IAS 20 *Accounting for government grants and disclosure of government assistance* requires the following accounting treatment.

Grants related to income

Either show as credit in the statement of profit or loss (other income) or deduct in reporting the related expense.

Grants related to assets

Treat as deferred income and credit to statement of profit or loss on systematic rational basis over useful life of asset **or** deduct grant in arriving at carrying value of asset and recognise as income over asset's life by means of reduced depreciation charge.

Disclose:

- Accounting policy

- Nature and extent of grants recognised

- Unfulfilled conditions and other contingencies relating to grants recognised

Recognise only when reasonable assurance that any conditions will be met and monies received.

Investment Property is property held to earn rentals or for capital appreciation or both, rather than for:

(a) use in the production or supply of goods or services or for administrative purposes

(b) sale in the ordinary course of business

Owner-occupied property cannot be classified as investment property.

Accounting treatment

An entity can choose to hold investment property under either:

(a) the fair value model; or

(b) the cost model

This choice will apply to **all** of its investment property.

IAS 23 *Borrowing costs*

The standard deals with borrowing costs for **self-constructed assets**.

Borrowing costs

Interest and other costs incurred by an entity in connection with the borrowing of funds.

Qualifying asset

An asset that necessarily takes a substantial period of time to get ready for its intended sale or use.

Included in borrowing costs

- Interest on bank overdrafts and short and long term borrowings
- Amortisation of discounts or premiums related to borrowings
- Amortisation of ancillary costs incurred with the arrangement of borrowings
- Finance charges in respect of finance leases under IAS 17
- Exchange differences as far as they are an adjustment to interest costs

Capitalisation is **mandatory** if the costs are **directly attributable** to the acquisition, construction or production of a qualifying asset.

Notes

5: Impairment of assets

Topic List

IAS 36

IAS 36 covers impairment of assets.

The aim of IAS 36 *Impairment of assets* is to ensure that assets are carried in the financial statements at no more than their **recoverable amount.** Note that IAS 36 does not apply to non-current assets held for sale, which are covered by IFRS 5.

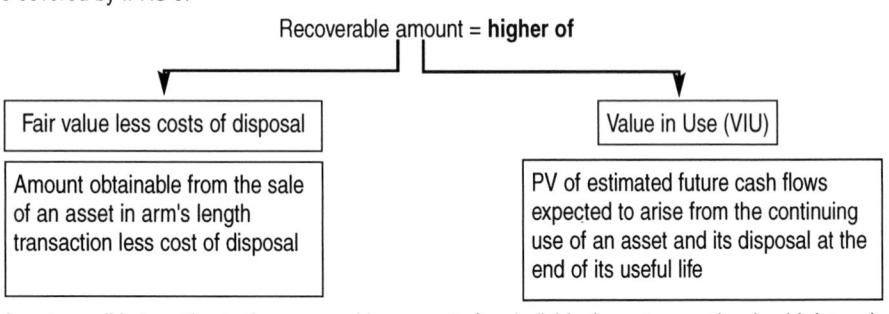

Recoverable amount = **higher of**

Fair value less costs of disposal	Value in Use (VIU)
Amount obtainable from the sale of an asset in arm's length transaction less cost of disposal	PV of estimated future cash flows expected to arise from the continuing use of an asset and its disposal at the end of its useful life

Where it is not possible to estimate the recoverable amount of an individual asset, an entity should determine the recoverable amount of the **cash-generating unit** to which it belongs.

The standard also specifies when an entity should reverse an impairment loss and prescribes certain disclosures for impaired assets.

Indicators of impairment

External indicators	Internal indicators
■ Fall in market value	■ Obsolescence or physical damage
■ Change in technological, legal or economic environment	■ Adverse changes in use
■ Increase in market interest rate likely to affect discount rates	■ Adverse changes in asset's economic performance
■ Carrying amount of entity's net assets > market capitalisation	

It may not be possible to associate cash flows with individual assets so the review of the recoverable amount will often have to be applied to **cash generating units** that contain groups of related assets.

Calculation of value in use

Include cash flows	Exclude cash flows
■ Directly attributable	■ Any future restructuring to which the entity is not yet committed
■ An appropriate proportion that can be allocated on a reasonable and consistent basis	■ Future capital expenditure that will improve/enhance asset in excess of originally assessed standard of performance
■ Net cash flows to be received or paid for the disposal of the asset at the end of its useful life on a fair value basis	■ Financing activities
	■ Income tax receipts or payments

The discount rate should be a pre-tax rate that reflects current market assessments of the time value of money and the risks specific to the asset.

Allocation of impairment loss

1 To the goodwill allocated to the cash generating unit

2 To all other assets in the cash generating unit on a pro rata basis

Recognition of losses

- Assets carried at historic cost – profit or loss

- Revalued assets – under rules of applicable IFRS

- Depreciation adjusted in future periods to allocate the asset's revised carrying amount less residual value over its remaining useful life

Reversal of past impairments

Where the recoverable amount increases, the resulting reversal should be recognised in the current period to the extent that it increases the carrying amount up to the amount that it would have been (net of amortisation or depreciation) had no impairment loss been recognised in prior years.

- **Individual assets:** recognise as income immediately in the statement of profit or loss and other comprehensive income unless the asset is carried at revalued amount under another IFRS in which case apply the rules of that IFRS

- **CGUs:** exact opposite of its original recognition while ensuring that assets are not increased above the lower of their recoverable amount and their carrying amount (after depreciation or amortisation) had there been no impairment loss

- **Goodwill:** not reversed in subsequent period unless:
    - The impairment was caused by a specific external event of an exceptional nature not expected to recur
    - Subsequent external events have occurred which reverse the effect of that event

Disclosure

- The amount of impairment losses recognised in the statement of profit or loss and other comprehensive income during the period and the line items affected

- The amount of impairment loss reversals recognised in the statement of profit or loss and other comprehensive income during the period and the line items affected

- The amount of impairment losses debited directly against equity in the period

- The amount of impairment loss reversals credited directly to equity in the period for material impairment losses or loss reversals:

    - The events and circumstances

    - The amount

    - The nature of the asset or cash generating unit

    - For initial losses whether recoverable amount is fair value less costs of disposal or VIU (and details of basis of selling price or discount rate as appropriate)

Notes

6: Accounting for leases

Leasing transactions are common in practice. It is important that you get to grips with IAS 17 as it is highly examinable.

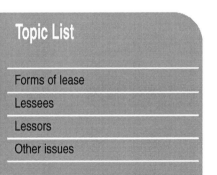

Topic List

Forms of lease

Lessees

Lessors

Other issues

Finance lease

- Transfers substantially all the risks and rewards of ownership of an asset to the lessee; title may or may not be transferred

- Comparison of present value of minimum lease payments and fair value of leased asset is commonly used to judge whether risks and rewards have been transferred (no numerical guidance in IFRS)

- **PV:** calculate using the interest rate implicit in the lease

Operating lease

A lease other than a finance lease

- Minimum lease payments are the payments over the lease term that the lessee is, or can be required to make (excluding contingent rent, costs for services and taxes to be paid by and reimbursed to the lessor), and

  - Lessee any amounts guaranteed by him or a party related to him

  - Lessor any residual value guaranteed to lessor by lessee, party related to lessee or independent third party

- **Lease term:** the period for which the lessee has contracted to lease the asset (primary **and** secondary periods)

Accounting treatment

- **Finance lease:** record as an asset and obligation at the lower of present value of the minimum lease payments and fair value
- The asset should be depreciated over the shorter of the lease term and its useful life
- A finance charge is made to produce a constant periodic rate of charge on the outstanding lease obligation (use actuarial method before tax and sum of the digits method)
- **Operating lease:** rentals charged on a straight-line basis over the lease term unless another systematic basis is representative of user's benefit

Disclosure

- Leased assets: net carrying amount at year end date
- Finance lease liabilities
  - Two disclosure notes
  - Reconciliation of minimum lease payments and PV
  - Breakdown of PV
  - For both, give maturity analysis (< 1 yr; 2–5 yrs; >5 yrs)
- Operating leases: future minimum lease payments under non-cancellable operating leases split < 1 yr, 2–5 yrs, > 5 yrs
- P/L (typical disclosures): depreciation charge on assets under finance leases, finance charge on finance leases, operating lease rentals, accounting policy

Lessors – accounting treatment

Finance lease

- Recognise receivable equal to net investment in the lease as a finance lease asset

- Mirror image of lessee's liability plus unguaranteed residual value

- Unguaranteed residual value is portion of residual value of asset not guaranteed by lessee or guaranteed only by party related to lessor

- Finance income recognised reflecting constant periodic rate of return on net investment outstanding

Operating lease

- Assets held for use under operating leases, are recorded as an asset on the SOFP and income in P/L on a straight line basis unless another systematic basis is more representative

Sale and leaseback transactions

- If leaseback is a **finance lease,** defer book profit/loss and amortise over lease term

  Double entry is:

  DEBIT   Cash

  CREDIT Finance lease liability

  and then as any other finance lease

- If leaseback transaction is an **operating lease;** where SP = sales proceeds; FV = fair value:

  - If SP = FV (see IFRS 13), recognise any profit/loss immediately

  - If SP < FV, recognise profit/loss immediately **unless** the apparent loss is compensated by future rentals at below market price, in which case defer and amortise

  - If SP > FV, defer the excess over FV and amortise over lease term (ie recognise FV minus Book Value)

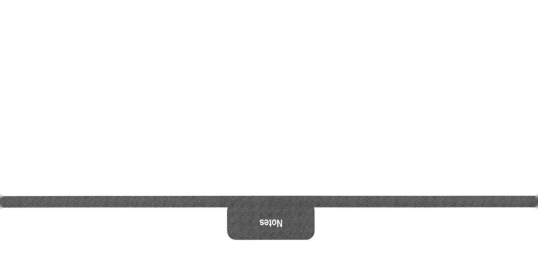

Notes

7: Intangible non-current assets and goodwill

Topic List

IAS 38

Goodwill

IAS 38 aims to prescribe the accounting treatment for intangible assets not dealt with under another IAS. The standard deals with the criteria for recognition and measurement.

Goodwill is a controversial area. It comes up again in connection with group accounts.

Definition

An intangible asset is an identifiable non-monetary asset without physical substance held for use in the production or supply of goods or services, for rental to others, or for administrative purposes.

Recognition

Recognise if and only if:

- It is probable that the future economic benefits that are attributable to the asset will flow to the entity

- The cost of the asset can be measured reliably

Initial measurement

Intangible assets should initially be measured at cost.

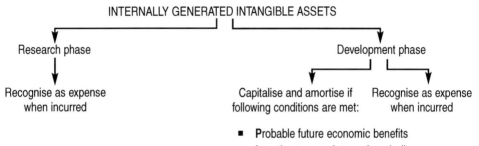

INTERNALLY GENERATED INTANGIBLE ASSETS

Research phase

Recognise as expense
when incurred

Development phase

Capitalise and amortise if
following conditions are met:

Recognise as expense
when incurred

- **P**robable future economic benefits
- **I**ntention to complete and use/sell
- **R**esources adequate to complete and use/sell
- **A**bility to use/sell
- **T**echnical feasibility
- **E**xpenditure can be reliably measured

Internally generated brands, mastheads, publishing titles, customer lists and similar items should not be recognised as intangible assets.

Subsequent expenditure

Subsequent expenditure must meet the original recognition criteria to be added to the cost of the intangible asset.

Amortisation

Should be charged on a systematic basis over the useful life of the asset. Should commence when asset available for use. Period and method to be reviewed at each year end.

Intangibles with indefinite useful life are not amortised, but reviewed at least annually for impairment.

Subsequent re-measurement

Cost model: cost less accumulated amortisation and impairment losses.

Revaluation model: revalued amount less subsequent accumulated amortisation and impairment losses.

Revalued amount is fair value at date of revaluation by reference to an active market.

All other assets in the same class should be revalued unless there is no active market for them, in which case the cost model value should be used for those assets.

Revaluations so that the carrying amount does not offer materially from fair value.

Impairment losses

The recoverable amount of the asset should be determined at least at each financial year end and any impairment loss should be accounted for in accordance with IAS 36.

Disclosures

Need to make the following disclosures.

- Distinguish between internally generated and other intangible assets
- Useful lives of assets and amortisation methods
- Gross carrying amount and accumulated amortisation at start and end of period
- Where the amortisation is included in the statement of profit or loss
- A reconciliation of opening balance to closing balance
- If research and development, how much was charged as expense

Goodwill can be purchased or be acquired as part of a business combination. In either case, the treatment is capitalisation at cost or fair value under IFRS 3.

Negative goodwill

Arises when acquirer's interest in identifiable net assets exceeds the cost of the combination. Results from **errors** or a **bargain**

Reassess cost of combination and assets

Recognise **any remaining** goodwill **immediately** in **profit or loss**

Goodwill

Future economic benefits arising from assets that are not capable of being individually identified and separately recognised

Recognise as an asset and measure at cost/excess of purchase cost over acquired interest

Do **not amortise**

Test at least annually for **impairment** (IAS 36)

You will be calculating goodwill as part of a group accounts question.

8: Inventories

Inventory is a relatively straightforward area, so only a brief summary is given here.

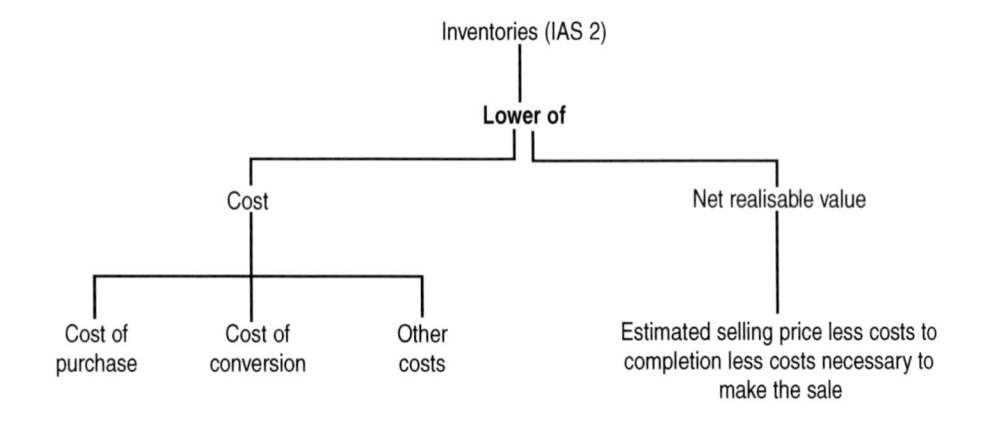

Permitted treatment of cost: FIFO or weighted average

LIFO is not permitted under IAS 2

9: Provisions, contingent liabilities and contingent assets

Topic List

IAS 37

IAS 37 should be familiar to you from your earlier studies. It is particularly topical in the light of increasing environmental awareness.

IAS 37

IAS 37 *Provisions, contingent liabilities and contingent assets* was brought in to remedy some abuses of provisions.

- Entities should **not provide** for **costs** that need to be incurred to **operate in the future,** if those **costs could be avoided** by the entity's future actions

- **Costs of restructuring** are to be recognised as a provision only when the entity has an **obligation** to carry out the restructuring

- The **full amount** of any **decommissioning costs** or environmental liabilities should be **recognised from the date on which they arise**

Provision

A liability of uncertain timing or amount. Liabilities are obligations to transfer economic benefits as a result of past transactions or events.

Contingent liability

Should be disclosed unless the possibility of any outflow of economic benefits to settle it is remote.

Contingent asset

Should be disclosed where an inflow of economic benefits is probable.

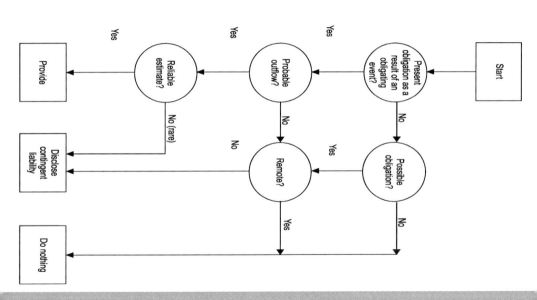

9: Provisions, contingent liabilities and contingent assets

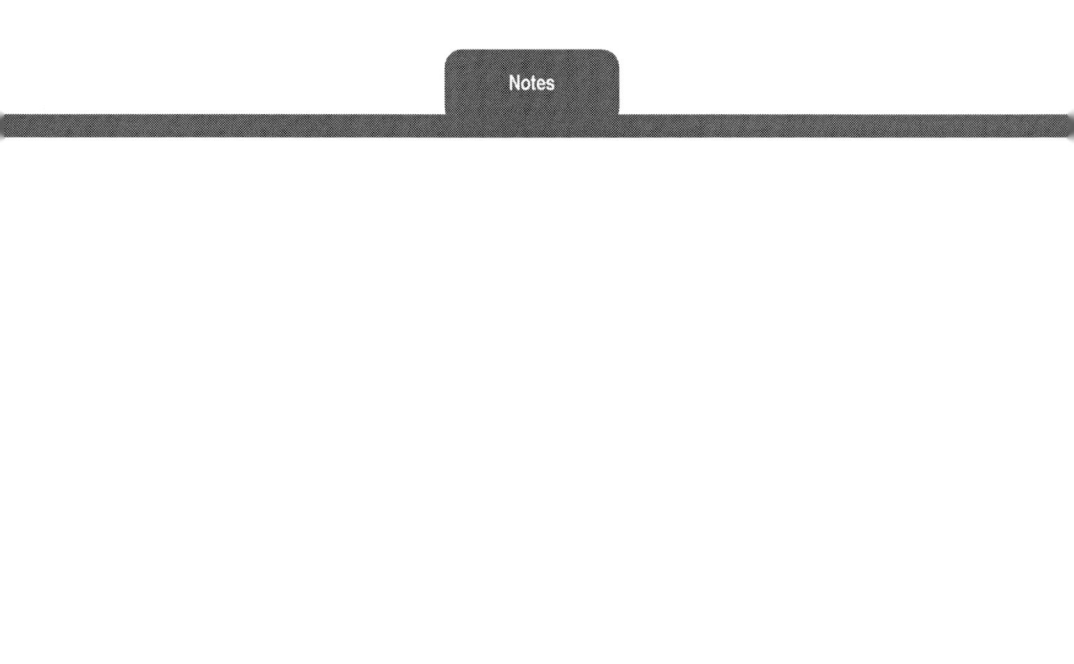

10: Employee benefits

IAS 19 Employee benefits *is likely to be tested as part of a longer question rather than as a full question.*

IAS 19

IAS 19 *Employee benefits* deals with all employee benefits, not just pensions.

Objectives

An entity should recognise an expense as it consumes the economic benefits of employee service in exchange for employee benefits and a liability where these are to be paid in the future.

Examples – Short-term benefits

- Wages, salaries and social security contributions
- Paid annual/sick leave
- Profit sharing and bonuses (if payable within 12 months of year end)
- Non-monetary benefits (eg health care, accommodation etc)

Accounting treatment

- Recognise expense on an accruals basis (undiscounted)
- Short-term **accumulating** compensated absences (eg unused holiday carried forward) are recognised when the employee renders service increasing entitlement to compensated absences
- Short-term **non-accumulating** compensated absences (eg maternity pay) are recognised when the absences occur

Retirement benefits

Defined contribution plans are post-employment benefit plans under which an entity pays fixed contributions into a separate entity (a fund) and will have no legal or constructive obligation to pay further contributions if the fund does not hold sufficient assets to pay all employee benefits relating to employee service in current and prior periods.

Defined benefit plans are post-employment plans other than defined contribution plans.

Defined contribution plans

- The company's only obligation is to pay the agreed amount (normally a percentage of salary) into a plan on behalf of its employee

- *Accounting treatment:* charge contributions payable in respect of the accounting period; if amounts paid are different, then a prepayment/accrual will appear

- *Disclosure:* expense recognised for period

10: Employee benefits

Defined benefit plans

- Role of actuary: calculates P/L charge for year; provides rate of expected return on assets and discount rate for liabilities (interest cost); values the assets and liabilities of pension fund, determines contributions required
- Accounted for by actuary measuring the liability using the projected unit credit method

Defined benefit plans

- The projected unit credit method sees each period of service as giving rise to an additional unit of benefit entitlement and measures each unit separateey to build up the final obligation

A suggested approach

Cost	Recognise
Interest cost on obligation	Increase in present value of defined benefit obligation because benefits are one year closer to payment. The discount rate is determined by reference to market yields on high quality fixed-rate corporate bonds. It is applied to the net defined benefit at the start of the accounting period. Debit Interest cost ($x\% \times$ b/d obligation) (P/L) Credit PV defined benefit obligation (SOFP)

Interest on plan assets	Long-term expected increase in assets based on discount rate (determined as for interest cost on obligation) and applied to b/d assets.
	DEBIT Plan assets (SOFP) CREDIT Expected return (x% × b/d assets) (P/L)
	(Technically the expected return is also time apportioned on contributions less benefits paid in year)
Current service costs	Increase in the present value of defined benefit obligation as the result of employee service in the current period (provided by the actuary, but may need to be discounted back to period end).
	DEBIT Current service cost (P/L) CREDIT PV defined benefit obligation (SOFP)
Gains and losses on settlement	Difference between the value of the obligation being settled and the settlement price
	Gain DEBIT PV defined benefit obligation (SOFP) CREDIT Service cost (P/L)
	Loss DEBIT Service cost (P/L) CREDIT PV defined benefit obligation (SOFP)

10: Employee benefits

Remeasurements: actuarial gains and losses	■ Arising from annual valuations of obligation ■ On obligation, differences between actuarial assumptions and actual experience during the period, or changes in actuarial assumptions
	Gain DEBIT PV defined benefit obligation (SOFP) CREDIT Other comprehensive income (SPLOCI)
	Loss DEBIT Other comprehensive income (SPLOCI) CREDIT PV defined benefit obligation (SOFP)
Remeasurements: return on assets	Arising from annual valuations of plan assets
	Gain DEBIT FV plan assets (SOFP) CREDIT Other comprehensive income (SPLOCI)
	Loss DEBIT Other comprehensive income (SPLOCI) CREDIT FV plan assets (SOFP)

Treatment of remeasurements (actuarial gain/loss)

IAS 19 requires actuarial gains and losses, now called remeasurements, to be recognised in the period incurred.

They are recognised in other comprehensive income and not reclassified to profit or loss for the year.

Calculation of actuarial gain/loss

Market value of plan assets		Present value of obligation	
	$m		$m
Market value of plan assets b/d	X	PV of obligation at start of year	X
Interest on plan assets (x%)	X	Interest cost (x%)	X
Contributions	X	Current service cost	X
Benefits paid	(x)	Past service cost	X
Settlements	(x)	Benefits paid	(x)
Return on plan assets: bal. figure	X	Settlements	(x)
Market value of plan assets c/d	X̄	Actuarial (gain)/loss on obligation: bal. fig.	X
		PV of obligation at end of year	X̄

11: Financial instruments

Topic List

Financial instruments

IAS 32

IFRS 9

IFRS 9 changes

IFRS 7

Fair value measurement

This is a controversial and complex topic. It is also the subject of recent significant change as IFRS 9 has replaced IAS 39.

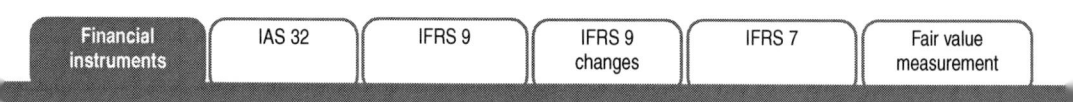

Financial instrument

Any contract that gives rise to a financial asset of one entity and a financial liability or equity instrument of another.

Relevant standards

IAS 32 deals with the classification of instruments as debt or equity.

IFRS 9 (July 2014) has replaced IAS 39 and deals with recognition, measurement, impairment and hedging.

IFRS 7 provides disclosure requirements for financial instruments.

Financial asset

Cash; equity instrument of another entity; contractual right to receive cash/other financial assets; contract that can be settled in the entity's own equity instruments and may be either a derivative or a non-derivative.

Financial liability

Contractual obligation to deliver cash/other financial asset; contractual obligation to exchange financial instruments under potentially unfavourable conditions.

Equity instrument

Contract that evidences a residual interest in the assets of an entity after deducting all its liabilities.

IAS 32 presentation

- An issuer of financial instruments should classify them as either
  - Liability (debt) or
  - Equity
- Compound instruments (exhibiting characteristics of both) must be split into their debt and equity components
- Substance rather than legal form applies (eg redeemable preference shares are a financial liability)
- Interest, dividends, loss or gains relating to a financial instrument classified as a liability are reported in the SPLOCI, while distributions to holders of equity instruments are debited directly to equity (in the SOCE)
- Offset of a financial asset and liability is only allowed where there is a legally enforceable right and the entity intends to settle net or simultaneously

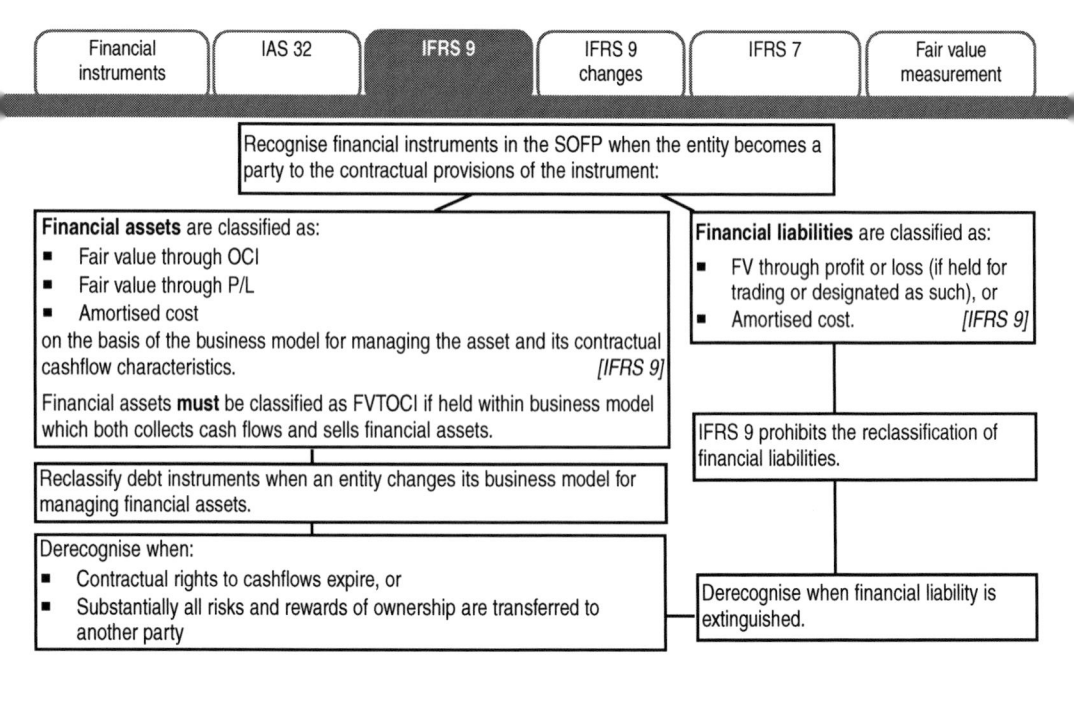

Recognise financial instruments in the SOFP when the entity becomes a party to the contractual provisions of the instrument:

Financial assets are classified as:
- Fair value through OCI
- Fair value through P/L
- Amortised cost

on the basis of the business model for managing the asset and its contractual cashflow characteristics. *[IFRS 9]*

Financial assets **must** be classified as FVTOCI if held within business model which both collects cash flows and sells financial assets.

Reclassify debt instruments when an entity changes its business model for managing financial assets.

Derecognise when:
- Contractual rights to cashflows expire, or
- Substantially all risks and rewards of ownership are transferred to another party

Financial liabilities are classified as:
- FV through profit or loss (if held for trading or designated as such), or
- Amortised cost. *[IFRS 9]*

IFRS 9 prohibits the reclassification of financial liabilities.

Derecognise when financial liability is extinguished.

	Initial measurement	Subsequent measurement	Related income/expense
Financial assets at amortised cost	FV of consideration given + transaction costs	Initial measurement – principal repayments +/– cumulative amortisation – impairments	Interest income (received + 'winding up') is recognised in profit or loss
Financial assets at fair value	FV of consideration given	Remeasured to FV at each period end	Changes in FV are recognised in – Profit or loss – OCI if business model achieved by collecting cash flows and selling financial assets – OCI if asset is equity instrument not held for trading and election made
Financial liabilities at amortised cost	FV of consideration received – transaction costs	Initial measurement – principal repayments +/– cumulative amortisation – impairments	Interest expense (paid + 'winding up') is recognised in profit or loss
Financial liabilities at FVTPL	FV of consideration received	Remeasured to FV at each period end	Changes in FV of financial liabilities held for trading are recognised in profit or loss

The change in FV of a financial liability DESIGNATED as FVTPL is split into two elements:

– Gain or loss from credit risk ⟶ recognise in OCI
– Other gain or loss ⟶ recognise in profit or loss

Amortised cost – Example

The method used in the following example applies to deep discount bonds and other similar instruments (including zero coupon bonds).

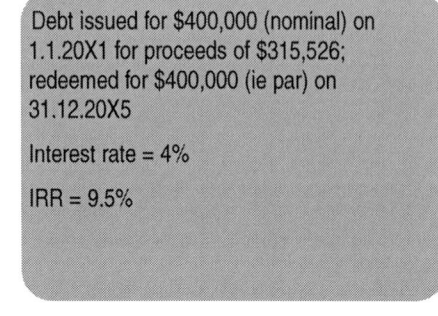

Debt issued for $400,000 (nominal) on 1.1.20X1 for proceeds of $315,526; redeemed for $400,000 (ie par) on 31.12.20X5

Interest rate = 4%

IRR = 9.5%

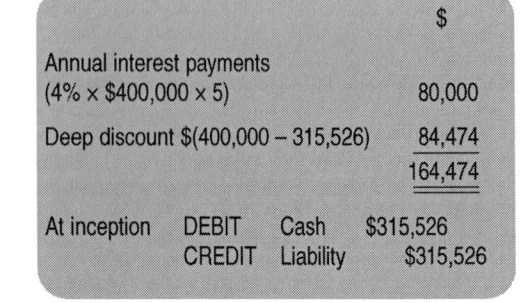

			$
Annual interest payments (4% × $400,000 × 5)			80,000
Deep discount $(400,000 – 315,526)			84,474
			164,474
At inception	DEBIT	Cash	$315,526
	CREDIT	Liability	$315,526

Year	P/L charge *$	Actual interest payable $	Winding up interest charged to P/L $	Liability in closing SOFP $
20X1	29,975	16,000	13,975	329,501
20X2	31,303	16,000	15,303	344,804
20X3	32,756	16,000	16,756	361,560
20X4	34,348	16,000	18,348	379,908
20X5	36,092	16,000	20,092	400,000
	164,474	80,000	84,474	

*9.5% × opening liability in SOFP

Fair value is measured as quoted market price in an active market where possible.

Overview

Impairment

- Impairment review where evidence of financial asset being impaired

- Expended credit loss model used

- Impairment loss is charged to P/L

- Where financial asset suffers impairment loss, cumulative losses on fair value adjustments previously recognised in equity are reclassified to P/L as well as impairment loss

- Reversal: P/L

Embedded derivatives

= Derivatives embedded within a host contract, eg construction contract in foreign currency

HOST ≠ FINANCIAL ASSET
Separate derivative from host and account for as a derivative when conditions are met.
Account for host contract as normal.

HOST = IFRS 9 FINANCIAL ASSET
Account for hybrid contract in accordance with IFRS 9

Hedging

Hedge accounting is mandatory where a transaction qualifies as a hedge (all criteria met):

- Economic relationship between the hedged item and the hedging instrument

- Effect of credt risk does not dominate value changes from the economic relationship

- Hedge ratio of hedging relationship is the same as that resulting from the quantity of the hedged item that the entity acutally hedges

IFRS 9 identifies three types of hedges which determines their accounting treatment.

Type	Hedges against	Accounting treatment
Fair value hedge	Changes in fair value of a recognised asset or liability or an unrecognised firm commitment* (or portion of either) that could affect profit or loss	■ Gain or loss on instrument is recognised in the P/L ■ Gain or loss on hedged item also recognised in P/L (and adjusts the carrying value of hedged item)
Cash flow hedge	Exposure to variability in cash flows attributable to a risk associated with a recognised asset or liability that could affect profit or loss	■ Gain or loss on effective portion of instrument is recognised in other comprehensive income (and recognised in P/L when asset or liability affects profit or loss, eg by interest income) ■ Gain or loss on ineffective portion is recognised in P/L
Hedge of net investment in a foreign operation	Variability in value of the net investment in a foreign operation or monetary items accounted for as part of that net investment	As for cash flow hedge

*IFRS 9 allows the hedge of a foreign currency firm commitment to be accounted for as a cash flow hedge.

IFRS 9 expected credit loss model

IFRS 9 used an **incurred loss model** for the impairment of financial assets. This assumed all loans will be repaid unless there is evidence to the contrary. This changed in the final version of IFRS 9 to an expected credit loss model.

- Effective interest rate to include an initial estimate of expected credit losses (therefore they are spread over instrument's life)
- Credit losses held in a separate allowance account (a reconciliation is disclosed)
- Losses due to changes in cash flow estimates disclosed as a separate line item
- 'Write-offs' direct to Financial Asset account if considered uncollectible
- Disclosures to show effect of credit losses, reconciliation of non-performing financial assets and results of any stress testing

Amount of impairment

The amount of the impairment to be recognised on these financial instruments **depends on whether or not they have significantly deteriorated** since their initial recognition.

Stage 1   Financial instruments whose credit quality has not significantly deteriorated since their initial recognition

Stage 2   Financial instruments whose credit quality has significantly deteriorated since their initial recognition

Stage 3   Financial instruments for which there is objective evidence of an impairment as at the reporting date

For stage 1 financial instruments, the impairment represents the present value of expected credit losses that will result if a default occurs in the 12 months after the reporting date **(12 months expected credit losses)**.

For financial instruments classified as stage 2 or 3, an impairment is recognised at the present value of expected credit shortfalls over their remaining life **(lifetime expected credit loss)**. Entities are required to reduce the gross carrying amount of a financial asset in the period in which they no longer have a reasonable expectation of recovery.

IFRS 9 Hedging changes

Under the final version of IFRS 9 the 80%–125% 'bright line' test of whether a hedging relationship qualifies for hedge accounting was replaced by an **objective-based assessment**:

- This allows genuine hedging relationships to be accounted for as such whereas the old IAS 39 rules sometimes **prevented** management from **accounting** for an actual hedging transaction as a hedge

- **Fair value hedges**: the IAS 39 treatment of recognising both changes in the fair value of the hedged item and changes in value of the hedging instrument in profit or loss is retained, but rules changed so that hedges of investments of equity instruments held at fair value through other comprehensive income can be accounted for as hedges

- **Cash flow hedges**: will continue to be accounted for as under IAS 39. Hedging gains and losses recognised in other comprehensive income will be recognised in a separate cash flow hedge reserve in equity

The main disclosures required are:

Statement of financial position

- Carrying amount of financial assets and liabilities by IFRS 9 category
- Reasons for any reclassification between fair value and amortised cost
- Details of assets and exposure to risk where transfers of assets have taken place
- Carrying amount of financial assets pledged as collateral
- Allowance for credit losses
- Multiple embedded derivatives
- Defaults and breaches

Statement of profit or loss and other comprehensive income

- Net gains/losses by IFRS 9 category
- Interest income/expense
- Impairment losses by class of financial asset

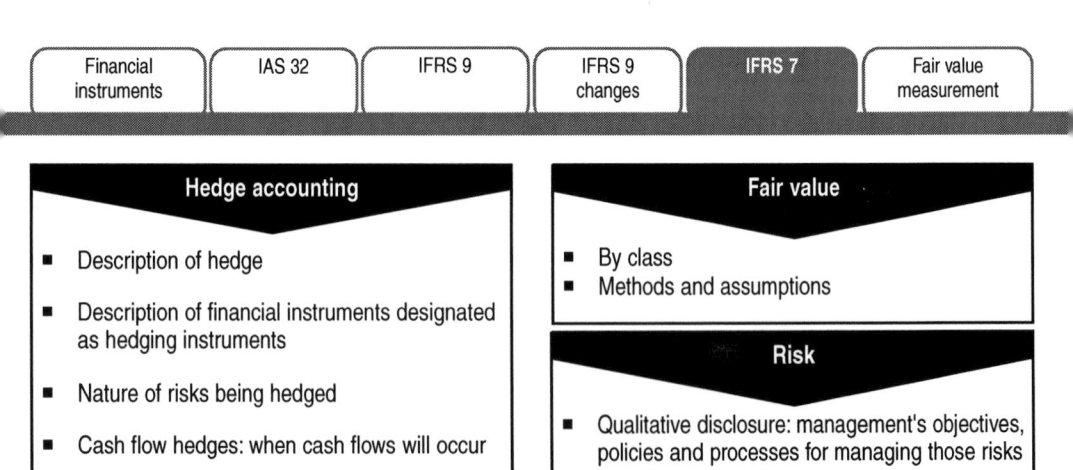

Hedge accounting

- Description of hedge
- Description of financial instruments designated as hedging instruments
- Nature of risks being hedged
- Cash flow hedges: when cash flows will occur
- FV hedges: gains or losses on hedged item and hedging instrument
- Ineffectiveness recognised in profit or loss

Fair value

- By class
- Methods and assumptions

Risk

- Qualitative disclosure: management's objectives, policies and processes for managing those risks
- Quantitative disclosure:
  - Extent of exposure to risk
  - Credit risk
  - Liquidity risk
  - Market risk

Fair value measurement

In May 2011 the IASB published IFRS 13 *Fair value measurement*. Its objective is to:

- Define fair value

- Set out in a single IFRS a framework for measuring fair value

- Require disclosure about fair value measurements

Fair value

The price that would be received to sell an asset or paid to transfer a liability in an orderly transaction between market participants at the measurement rate.

The rules of fair value measurement are brought together in IFRS 13 *Fair value measurement*.

IFRS 13

IFRS 13 states that valuation techniques must be those which are appropriate and for which sufficient data are available. Entities should maximise the use of relevant **observable inputs** and minimise the use of **unobservable inputs**.

The standard establishes a three-level hierarchy for the inputs that valuation techniques use to measure fair value:

Level 1   Quoted prices (unadjusted) in active markets for identical assets or liabilities that the reporting entity can access at the measurement date.

Level 2   Inputs other than quoted prices included within Level 1 that are observable for the asset or liability, either directly or indirectly, eg quoted prices for similar assets in active markets or for identical or similar assets in non active markets or use of quoted interest rates for valuation purposes.

Level 3   Unobservable inputs for the asset or liability, ie using the entity's own assumptions about market exit value.

12: Accounting for taxation

Topic List

Current tax

Deferred tax

Taxable temporary differences

Deductible temporary differences

Disclosure

In nearly all countries entities pay tax on their trading income. There are two aspects to this: current tax and deferred tax.

Most students find deferred tax more difficult than current tax, so study this section carefully.

IAS 12

IAS 12 covers both current and deferred tax. Current tax is fairly easy.

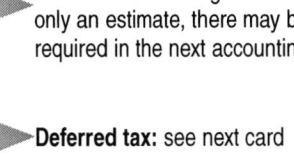

Tax charge	
Current tax	X
Under/overstatement of prior periods	X/(X)
Deferred tax	X
Share of tax of associates	X
	X

Current tax: an estimate of income tax payable for the current year

Under/overstatement of prior periods: as the income tax charge on taxable profits is only an estimate, there may be adjustments required in the next accounting period

Deferred tax: see next card

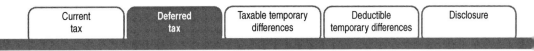

The tax charge in the statement of profit or loss often bears little relationship to the profit before tax figure because of the differences which exist between tax rules and financial accounting principles.

Accounting for deferred tax

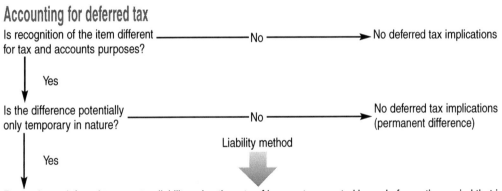

Is recognition of the item different for tax and accounts purposes? ———— No ————→ No deferred tax implications

Yes

Is the difference potentially only temporary in nature? ———— No ————→ No deferred tax implications (permanent difference)

Liability method

Yes

Recognise a deferred tax asset or liability using the rate of income tax enacted by end of reporting period that is expected to apply to the period when the asset is realised or the liability settled.

1 Temporary differences

Temporary timing differences arise as a result of the fact that certain items of income/expenditure are dealt with for tax purposes on a receipts basis and on an accruals basis for accounts purposes.

At the end of the reporting period, the timing difference is equivalent to the difference between the accrued income asset and the tax base of the income (amount received, ie nil).

2 Specific temporary differences – accelerated capital allowances

When tax (or 'capital') allowances/tax depreciation rates are available at a rate higher than the accounting depreciation rates applied to the same assets.

On a cumulative basis calculated as:

Carrying amount	X
Less tax written down value (TWDV)	(X)
	X

3 Revaluations

The revaluation of an asset will create a temporary difference when it is incorporated in the statement of financial position, insofar as the profit or loss that would result from realisation at the revalued amount is taxable. Deferred tax is normally provided out of the revaluation surplus.

Deductible temporary differences

Deductible temporary differences arise since certain items of expenditure are dealt with for tax purposes on a payments basis and on an accruals basis for accounts purposes.

At the end of the reporting period, the timing difference is equivalent to differences between the accrual and the tax base of the payment (amount paid, ie nil).

| Current tax | Deferred tax | Taxable temporary differences | Deductible temporary differences | Disclosure |

Disclosure

Statement of financial position

Deferred tax liability

Balance brought forward	X
Amount charged/(credited) to statement of profit or loss	X/(X)
Amount charged/(credited) to equity	X/(X)
Balance carried forward	X

Statement of profit or loss

Current tax	X
Under/overstatement of prior periods	X/(X)
Deferred tax	X
	X

13: Foreign currency translation

Topic List

IAS 21

Individual entity

There are two important concepts: functional currency and presentation currency. You need to know when and how to apply each.

Two currency concepts

Functional currency

- Currency of the primary economic environment in which an entity operates

- The currency used for measurement in the financial statements

- Other currencies treated as a foreign currency

Presentation currency

- Currency in which the financial statements are presented

- Special rules apply to translation from functional currency to presentation currency

- Same rules used for translating foreign operations

During the period

- Translate each transaction at **exchange rate on date of transaction** (average rate (AR) for a period may be used as an approximation, if rates do not fluctuate significantly)

- Where the transaction is settled during the period the exchange difference arising is a realised gain or loss and is reported in profit or loss for the year.

At the reporting date

- **Non-monetary assets held at historic cost** (non-current assets, inventory): remain at historical rate (HR)

- **Non-monetary assets held at fair value** (eg investments): exchange rate when fair value was determined

- **Monetary assets and liabilities:** restate at closing rate

Treatment of exchange differences

Part of profit/loss for the year

- On **trading transactions:** under 'other operating income or expense'

- On **financing transactions:** under 'finance income/finance cost'

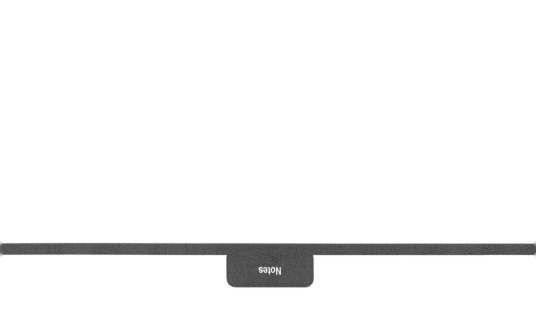

14: Accounting for agriculture and mineral resources

Topic List

IAS 41

IFRS 6

This chapter deals with the specific accounting requirements of agriculture and extractive industries.

IAS 41 deals with **biological assets** (defined as 'living plants and animals') from the point of their planting/birth until their harvest/slaughter:

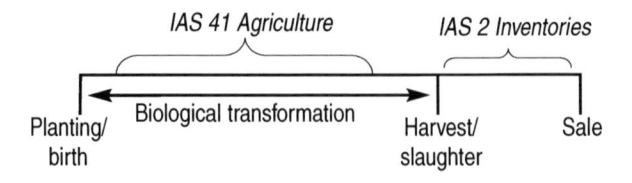

Biological transformation includes:

- Growth
- Degeneration, and
- Procreation

The scenario is that a company spends money searching for mineral resources to mine. How should it account for this expenditure?

Should it capitalise it – is there an asset? Or should it expense it?

The scope of IFRS 6 is very narrow. It only applies at a very specific point in time:

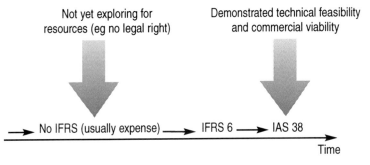

Not yet exploring for
resources (eg no legal right)

Demonstrated technical feasibility
and commercial viability

→ No IFRS (usually expense) → IFRS 6 → IAS 38

Time

14: Accounting for agriculture and mineral resources

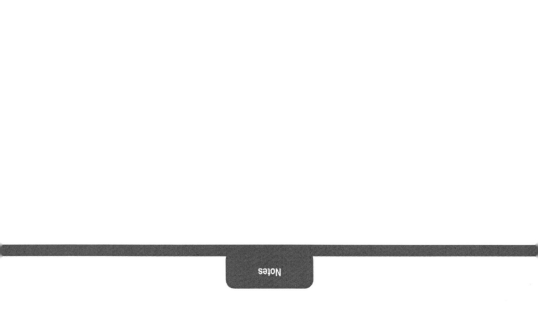
Notes

15: Share-based payment

Topic List

The issue

Types of transaction

The examiner tests this topic regularly, either as part of a longer question or as a question in its own right.

Share-based payments

Share-based payments are transactions whereby entities purchase goods and service from other parties, such as suppliers and employees, by issuing shares or share options.

The issue

This is a good example of substance over form (faithful representation). In the past when a limited liability company gave employees share options as remuneration, no expense was recognised in P/L.

This was believed to cause economic distortions and corporate governance concerns.

Two types of share-based payment transactions:

- **Equity settled** share-based payment transactions: the entity receives goods or services as consideration for **equity instruments** or the entity (including shares or share options).

- **Cash-settled** share-based payment transactions: the entity acquires goods or services by incurring **liabilities** to the supplier of those goods and services for amounts that are based on the price (or value) of the entity's shares or other equity instruments.

Recognition

DEBIT Expense (P/L)

CREDIT Equity (if equity-settled)

CREDIT Liability (if cash-settled)

Measurement

Equity-settled

Use the fair value of goods received **OR**

If these cannot be measured reliably, measure indirectly by reference to the fair value of the equity instruments granted.

Estimating fair value of equity instruments:

- Shares: market price at **grant date**
- Share options: use **option pricing model** to estimate fair value at grant date

Cash-settled

Eg share appreciation rights. Employees become entitled to a future **cash payment based on** the **increase** in the entity's **share price**.

Company must **recognise** services received and related liability **as services are rendered**. Liability must be recognised at fair value using an option pricing model. This fair value must be updated at each year end.

16: Presentation of published financial statements

Topic List

Statement of financial position

Statement of profit or loss and other comprehensive income

Changes in equity

Other matters

All of your studies for Dip IFR will be concerned with the accounts of limited liability companies, so it is important that you are familiar with the IAS 1 formats.

Statement of financial position (IAS 1 revised)

	20X7		20X6	
	$'000	$'000	$'000	$'000
Assets				
Non-current assets				
Property, plant & equipment	X		X	
Goodwill	X		X	
Other intangible assets	X		X	
Investments in associates	X		X	
Investments in equity instruments	X	X	X	X
Current assets				
Inventories	X		X	
Trade receivables	X		X	
Other current assets	X		X	
Cash and cash equivalents	X	X	X	X
Total assets		X		X
Equity and liabilities				
Equity attributable to owners of the parent				
Share capital	X		X	
Other reserves	X		X	
Retained earnings	X	X	X	X
Non-controlling interest	X		X	
Total equity		X		X
Non current liabilities				
Long-term borrowings	X		X	
Deferred tax	X		X	
Long-term provisions	X		X	
Total non-current liabilities		X		X
Current liabilities				
Trade and other payables	X		X	
Short term borrowings	X		X	
Current portion of long-term borrowings	X		X	
Current tax payable	X		X	
Short-term provisions	X		X	
Total current liabilities		X		X
Total equity and liabilities		X		X

Other matters

Changes in equity

Statement of profit or loss and other comprehensive income

Statement of financial position

Statement of profit or loss and other comprehensive income (IAS 1 revised)

	20X2 $'000	20X1 $'000
Revenue	X	X
Cost of sales	(X)	(X)
Gross profit	X	X
Other income	X	X
Distribution costs	(X)	(X)
Administrative expenses	(X)	(X)
Other expenses	(X)	(X)
Finance costs	(X)	(X)
Share of profit of associates	X	X
Profit before tax	X	X
Income tax expense	(X)	(X)
Profit for the year	X	X
Other comprehensive income:		
Investments in equity instruments	X	X
Gains on property revaluation	X	X
Income tax relating to components of other comprehensive income	(X)	(X)
Other comprehensive income for the year, net of tax	X	X
Total comprehensive income for the year	X	X
Profit attributable to:		
Owners of the parent	X	X
Non-controlling interest	X	X
	X	X
Total comprehensive income attributable to:		
Owners of the parent	X	X
Non-controlling interest	X	X
	X	X

Statement of changes in equity (IAS 1 revised)

	Share capital $'000	Retained earnings $'000	Revaluation surplus $'000	Total $'000	Non-controlling interest $'000	Total equity $'000
Balance at 1 January 20X6	X	X	X	X	X	X
Changes in accounting policy		X		X	X	X
Restated balance	X	X	X	X	X	X
Changes in equity for 20X6:						
Dividends		(X)		(X)		(X)
Total comprehensive income for the year		X	X	X	X	X
Balance at 31 December 20X6	X	X	X	X	X	X
Changes in equity for 20X7:						
Issue of share capital	X			X		X
Dividends		(X)		(X)		(X)
Total comprehensive income for the year		X	X	X	X	X
Transfer to retained earnings		X	(X)			
Balance at 31 December 20X7	X	X	X	X	X	X

IAS 1

The standard suggests that all sets of financial statements should apply the disclosures. An entity must explain all departures and, if relevant, why by following IAS/IFRS fair presentation is not achieved.

Current assets

- Expected to be realised/held for sale in normal course of entity's operating cycle

- Held for trading purposes and expected to be realised within 12 months

- Cash or cash equivalent asset not restricted in use

All other assets are non-current. Each entity must decide whether to present current/non-current assets/liabilities separately. If not, present them in order of liquidity.

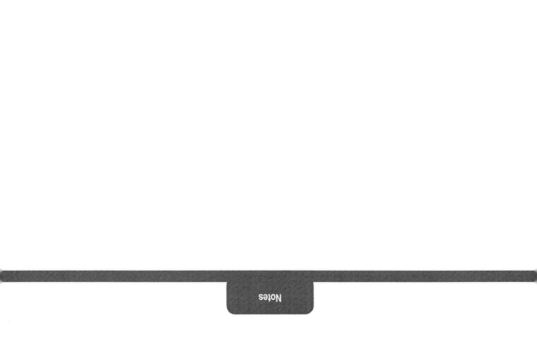

17: Reporting financial performance

Topic List

IAS 8

IFRS 5

This chapter is largely concerned with the income statement. There is no one single IAS concerned with reporting financial performance as there is in the UK.

IAS 8

Should include all items of income and expense for the period (ie not hidden in reserves) unless an IAS requires/permits otherwise.

Accounting policies

Accounting policies are the specific principles, bases, conventions, rules and practices applied by an entity in preparing and presenting financial statements.

An entity follows extant Standards and Interpretations when determining its accounting policies.

In the absence of a Standard or Interpretation covering a specific transaction, other event or condition, management uses its judgement to develop an accounting policy which results in information that is relevant and reliable, considering in the following order:

1. Standards or Interpretations dealing with similar and related issues
2. The *Conceptual Framework* definitions and recognition criteria
3. Other national GAAPs based on a similar conceptual framework (providing the treatment does not conflict with extant Standards, Interpretations or the *Conceptual Framework*).

Changes in accounting policy

Only allowed if:

Required by standard or interpretation

If the change will provide more relevant or reliable information about events or transactions

Accounting treatment:

Restate prior year statement of profit or loss and other comprehensive income and statement of financial position

Restate opening balance of retained earnings

Include as second line of SOCIE

Show effect on prior period at foot of prior year SOCIE

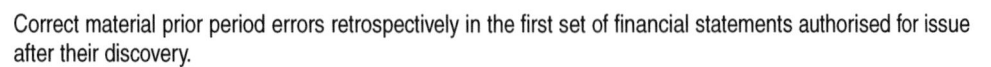

Changes in accounting estimates

Apply **prospectively**, ie in the current period (and future periods if also affected).

Prior period errors

Omissions from and misstatements in the entity's financial statements for one or more periods.

Correct material prior period errors retrospectively in the first set of financial statements authorised for issue after their discovery.

- Restate comparative amounts for each prior period presented in which the error occurred
- Restate the opening balances of assets, liabilities and equity for the earliest prior period presented
- Include any adjustment to opening equity as the second line of the statement of changes in equity
- Disclose the nature of the error and the amount of the correction to prior periods for each line item in each period affected

Where it is impracticable to determine the period-specific effects or the cumulative effect of the error, the entity corrects the error from the earliest period/date practicable (and discloses that fact).

IFRS 5 *Non-current assets held for sale and discontinued operations* was published in 2004.

Definitions

Discontinued operation	A component of an entity that either has been disposed of or is classified as held for sale and:
	(a) Represents a separate major line of business or geographical area of operations
	(b) Is part of a single co-ordinated plan to dispose of a separate major line of business or geographical area of operations, or
	(c) Is a subsidiary acquired exclusively with a view to resale
Component of an entity	Operations and cash flows that can be clearly distinguished, operationally and for financial reporting purposes, from the rest of the entity
Disposal group	A group of assets to be disposed of (by sale or otherwise) together as a group in a single transaction; **and** liabilities directly associated with those assets that will be transferred in the transaction
Asset held for sale	Its carrying amount will be recovered principally through sale rather than continuing use

17: Reporting financial performance

Non-current assets held for sale

Criteria

- The asset (or disposal group) must be available for immediate sale in its present condition, subject only to usual and customary sales terms and
- The sale must be highly probable.
  For this to be the case:
    - The appropriate level of **management** must be **committed** to a plan to sell;
    - An **active programme** to **locate a buyer** and complete the plan must have been initiated
    - The asset (or disposal group) must be **actively marketed** for sale at a price that is reasonable in relation to its current fair value
    - The sale should be expected to qualify for recognition as a completed sale **within one year** from the date of classification as held for sale (subject to limited specified exceptions)
    - Actions required to complete the plan should indicate that it is **unlikely** that **significant** changes to the plan will be made or that the plan will be withdrawn

Presentation

Assets and disposal groups (including associated liabilities) classified as held for sale are presented:

- On the face of the statement of financial position
- Separately from other assets and liabilities
- Normally as **current** assets and liabilities (not offset)

Measurement

An entity must measure a non-current asset or disposal group classified as held for sale at the **lower of**:

- Carrying amount
- Fair value less costs to sell

Immediately before initial classifications, measure asset per applicable IFRS. Any impairment loss accounted for as normal.

Non-current assets/disposal groups classified as held for sale are **not depreciated**.

Proforma disclosure

XYZ GROUP – STATEMENT OF PROFIT OR LOSS
FOR THE YEAR ENDED 31 DECEMBER 20X7

	20X7	20X6
	$'000	$'000
Continuing operations		
Revenue	X	X
Cost of sales	(X)	(X)
Gross profit	X	X
Other income	X	X
Distribution costs	(X)	(X)
Administrative expenses	(X)	(x)
Other expenses	(X)	(X)
Finance costs	(X)	(X)
Share of profit of associates	X	X
Profit before tax	X	X
Income tax expense	(X)	(X)
Profit for the year from continuing operations	X	X
Discontinued operations		
Profit for the year from discontinued operations	X	X
Profit for the year	X	X
Profit attributable to		
Owners of the parent	X	X
Non-controlling interest	X	X
	X	X

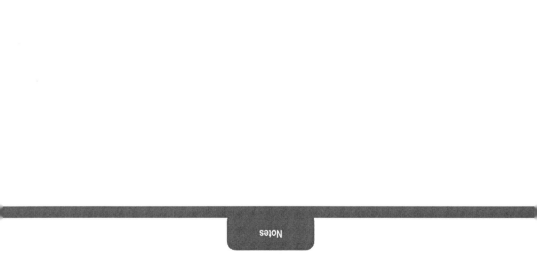

Notes

18: Earnings per share

Topic List

Basic EPS

Changes in capital structure

Diluted EPS

Earnings per share is a widely used measure of an entity's performance. It is useful for comparing the results of one entity over time and comparing the performance of an entity's equity against the performance of another entity's equity.

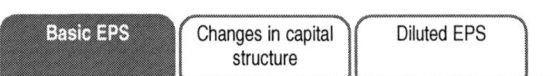

IAS 33

This standard aims to improve the **comparison** of different entities in the same period and of the same entity in different periods.

Basic calculation

Net profit/loss attributable to ordinary shareholders

Weighted average no. of shares in issue during the period

The net profit or loss used is after interest, tax and deductions in respect of non-equity shares.

Changes in capital structure

It is necessary to match the earnings for the year against the capital base giving rise to those earnings.

Bonus issue

The earnings of the entity will not rise (no new funds injected); to calculate the number of shares:

Treat bonus shares as if in issue for the full year

Apply retrospectively, reducing the reported EPS for the previous year by the reciprocal of the bonus fraction

Issue at full market price

New capital is introduced therefore earnings would be expected to rise from date of new issue; to calculate the number of shares:

Use time weighted average number of shares for period

No retrospective effect

Rights issue

For purposes of calculating the number of shares, treat this as an issue at full market price followed by a bonus issue:

Use weighted average number of shares in issue for the period modified by the retrospective effect of the bonus element

Bonus element

$$\frac{\text{Actual cum} - \text{rights price}}{\text{Theoretical ex} - \text{rights price}}$$

Diluted EPS

Required where a listed entity has outstanding convertible loan notes, preferred shares, debentures, options or warrants.

Must be shown on the face of the statement of profit or loss and given equal prominence with basic EPS.

- Numerators of calculations must be disclosed. Denominators must be disclosed and reconciled to each other

- Other amounts per share may be shown but profit used must be reconciled to a line item in the statement of profit or loss.

Convertible loan notes or preference shares

Earnings

Net basis earnings	X
Add back loan note interest net of tax (or preference dividends) 'saved'	X
Diluted earnings	X

No of shares

Basic weighted average	X
Add additional shares on conversion (use terms giving max dilution available after y/e)	X
Diluted number	X

19: Miscellaneous standards: related party disclosures and segment reporting

Topic List

Related party disclosures

Segment reporting

This topic could be tested either as a full question or part of a question.

Key elements: control, joint control, significant influence

A **person** is related to an entity if:

(1) They control or jointly control the entity (Mr A & B)

(2) They have significant influence over the entity (Mr A & C)

(3) They are key management personnel of the entity or its parent

(4) They are a close family member of any individual in (1)–(3)

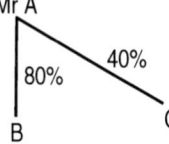

PLUS where an individual controls/jointly controls/has significant influence over two entities, they are related

An **entity** is related to another entity if:

(1) They are members of the same group (Z & Y)

(2) One is an associate or JV of the other (Z & X)

(3) Both are JVs of a third party (W & U)

(4) One is an associate and the other a JV of a third party (X & W)

(5) One is a pension plan for employees of the other

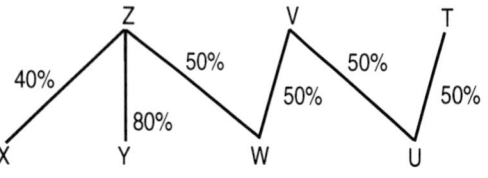

KEY FACTOR: SUBSTANCE OF RELATIONSHIP

Not necessarily related parties	Disclosure
■ Two entities simply because they have a director in common	Always
	(1) Name of parent + ultimate controlling party
■ Two venturers simply because they share joint control of a joint venture	(2) Key management personnel compensation
	Where RP transactions have occurred disclose for each category of related party
■ Providers of finance, trade unions, public utilities, government departments and agencies in the course of their normal dealings with an entity by virtue only of those dealings	(1) Nature of relationship
	(2) Amount of transactions
	(3) Amount of outstanding balances
■ A single customer, supplier, franchisor, distributor or general agent with whom an entity transacts a significant volume of business merely by virtue of the resulting economic dependence	(4) Provision for doubtful debts
	(5) Bad debt expense re related parties

Reasons for segment information

- Explains factors which have contributed to company results
- Users can compare results of different products year/year
- Users can compare performance with competitors
- Users can assess future risks and rewards

IFRS 8 *Operating segments*

- **Segment reporting** is necessary for a better understanding and assessment of:

  - Past performance
  - Risks and returns

- IFRS 8 adopts the **managerial approach** to identifying segments

- The standard gives guidance on how segments should be **identified** and **what information should be disclosed** for each

- It also sets out requirements for related disclosures about **products and services**, **geographical areas and major customers**

20: Reporting for small and medium-sized entities

Topic List

Big GAAP/Little GAAP

IFRS for SMEs

Areas of difference

Most companies are small, and have different accounting needs from the larger, listed companies for which IFRS was largely designed.

Big GAAP/Little GAAP

Most companies are **small**, owned and managed by one person or family.

Should there be two GAAPs?

- Simple for smaller companies
- More detailed for longer ones

In the UK, the **FRSSE** was developed for small companies, ie companies below certain legally defined limits. In 2009, the IASB published the IFRS for SMEs.

Possible solutions

- Differential reporting (standards specifically for smaller entities)
- Exemptions from IFRS or some requirements of IFRS

IFRS for Small and Medium-sized Entities

- Published July 2009
- Applies to companies **without public accountability** (rather than using a size test)
- Much **less guidance** than full IFRS
- **Simplified recognition** and **measurement** rules
- **Only one option** where full IFRS gives a choice
- Topics **irrelevant** to SMEs **omitted**
- Significantly **fewer disclosures**
- Written in **clear language**

Advantages: simpler, clearer, more relevant

Disadvantages: still onerous for very small companies, scope too wide, and there is room for further simplification

Key areas of difference – test yourself (look back to the text if you need to)

- Presentation and disclosure
- Financial instruments
- Investment property
- Property, plant and equipment
- Intangible assets
- Investments in subsidiaries and associates in the consolidated and separate accounts of the investor
- Government grants
- Borrowing costs
- Impairment of assets

21: Constitution of a group

Topic List

Group accounts

IFRS 10

Consolidation is a very important area of your Dip IFR syllabus, as you will get a 40-mark compulsory question on this in the examination.

This chapter looks at the basic definitions and relevant accounting standards.

Subsidiary

An entity that is controlled by another entity

Control: An investor controls an investee when the investor is exposed, or has rights, to variable returns from its involvement with the investee and has the ability to affect those returns through power over the investee.

Associate

An entity in which an investor has significant influence

Significant influence: the power to participate in the financial and operating policy decisions of an economic activity but not control over those policies.

These definitions are very important in dealing with group accounts. Make sure you understand them.

Summary of classification and treatment

Investment	Criteria	Required treatment in group accounts
Subsidiary	Control (>50% rule)	Full consolidation
Associate	Significant influence (20% + rule)	Equity accounting
Investment which is none of the above	Assets held for accretion of wealth	As for single entity accounts

Other provisions of IFRS 10

Consolidated financial statements:

The financial statements of a group presented as those of a single economic entity

Exemption
A parent need not prepare group accounts if: ■ It is itself a wholly owned subsidiary ■ It is partially owned and the other owners do not object. ■ Its securities are not publicly traded ■ The ultimate or intermediate parent publishes IFRS-compliant consolidated accounts

Other
■ Different reporting dates – adjustments should be made ■ Uniform accounting policies – if not, disclose why. Adjustments should be made on consolidation

22: The consolidated statement of financial position

Topic List

Consolidated statement of financial position

NCI

Method

Fair values

This chapter introduces the basic techniques you will need to prepare a consolidated statement of financial position.

Consolidated statement of financial position	NCI	Method	Fair values

Purpose	To show the assets and liabilities which it controls and their ownership
Assets and liabilities	Always 100% P plus S providing P has control
Share capital	P only
Reason	Simply reporting to the parent's shareholders in another form
Retained earnings	100% P plus group share of post-acquisition retained reserves of S less consolidation adjustments
Reason	To show the extent to which the group actually owns assets and liabilities included in the statement of financial position
Non-controlling interest	NCI share of S's consolidated assets less liabilities **or** fair value*
Reason	To show the extent to which other parties own assets and liabilities but under the control of the parent

NCI

IFRS 3 gives the option to value the non-contolling interest at **fair value**. This affects the goodwill and non-controlling interest calculations. The details are as follows: [P holds 60% of S. Goodwill impaired by $100,000 Fair value of NCI $900,000]

Non-controlling interest at share of net assets

Goodwill	$'000
Consideration transferred	1,600
Group share of net assets (2,000 × 60%)	(1,200)
Goodwill	400
Impairment	(100)
Carrying value	300

Non-controlling interest at fair value

Goodwill	$ '000
Consideration transferred	1,600
Fair value of NCI	900
Net assets	(2,000)
Goodwill	500
Impairment	(100)
Carrying amount	400

Note that the total goodwill is now $400,000, reflecting the $100,000 goodwill attributable to the non-controlling interest.

Non-controlling interest at end of reporting period

The option to value the non-contolling interest at fair value applies to non-controlling interest **at acquisiton**. However, it will affect the valuation of non-controlling interest **at the year end**.

Under the two options above, this will be as follows (net assets now $3m)

Non-controlling interest at share of net assets		**Non-controlling interest at fair value**	
	$'000		$'000
S net assets	3,000	Fair value of NCI	900
NCI 40%	1,200	NCI share of increase	
		Increase in net assets	
		((3,000 – 2000) × 40%)	400
		Goodwill impairment	
		(100 × 40%)	(40)
			1,260

Fair value options

If you are required to account for NCI at fair value there are two options:

(1) You may be told what fair value of the NCI is

(2) You may be given the share price at the date of acquisition

The examiner has said that he will usually examine NCI at FV, so be prepared for this.

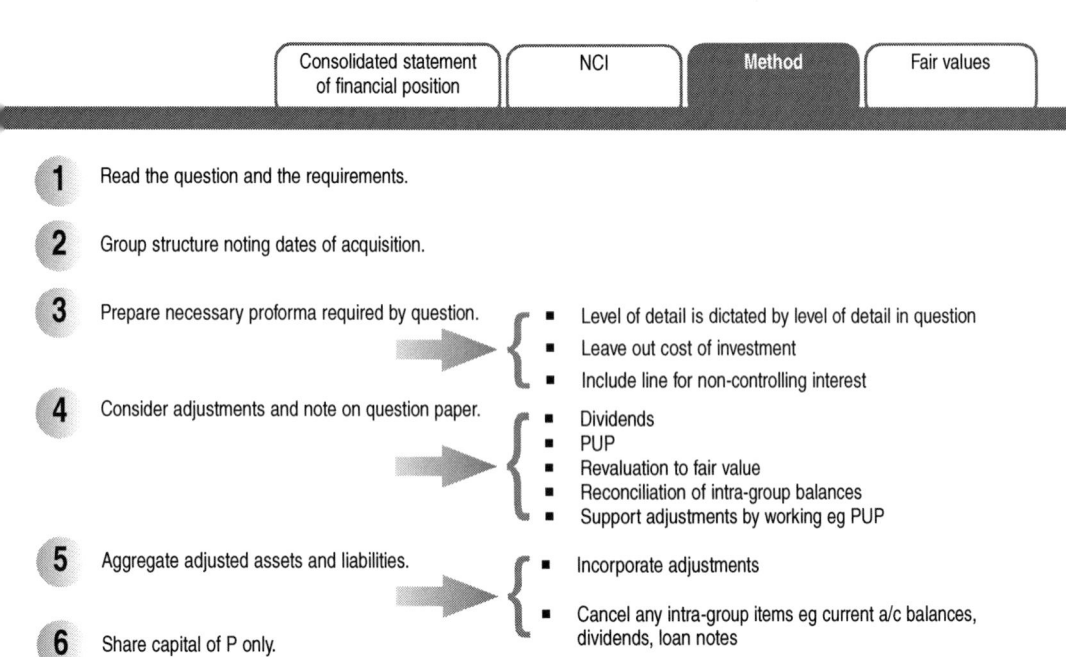

1. Read the question and the requirements.

2. Group structure noting dates of acquisition.

3. Prepare necessary proforma required by question.
   - Level of detail is dictated by level of detail in question
   - Leave out cost of investment
   - Include line for non-controlling interest

4. Consider adjustments and note on question paper.
   - Dividends
   - PUP
   - Revaluation to fair value
   - Reconciliation of intra-group balances
   - Support adjustments by working eg PUP

5. Aggregate adjusted assets and liabilities.
   - Incorporate adjustments
   - Cancel any intra-group items eg current a/c balances, dividends, loan notes

6. Share capital of P only.

	7	Goodwill			
		Consideration transferred		X	
		Non-controlling interest		X	
		Net assets acquired as represented by			
		Share capital	X		
		Share premium	X		
		Reserves	X		
		Retained earnings	X		
				(X)	
		Goodwill (gain on bargain purchase)		X/(X)	

> Remember that goodwill is retained in the statement, subject to impairment reviews. Remember rules for gain on a bargain purchase.

	8	Retained earnings		
			P	S
		Per question	X	X
		Adjustments as noted on question paper	X/(X)	X/(X)
			X	Y
		Share of S post acquisition %	X	
			X	
		Any impairment of goodwill	(X)	
			X	

22: The consolidated statement of financial position

9 Non-controlling interest

Fair value at acquisition	X
Share of post-acquisition retained earnings (per 8)	X
Share of any goodwill impairment	(X)
	X

Note. Negative goodwill would be credited to the statement of profit or loss as a 'gain on a bargain purchase'.

Fair values (IFRS 3)

On consolidation, the **fair value** of the consideration paid for a subsidiary is compared with the **fair value** of the identifiable assets and liabilities acquired. Fair value is determined in accordance with IFRS 13, which was covered in Chapter 11.

Fair value

The price that would be received to sell an asset or paid to transfer a liability in an orderly transaction between market participants at the measurement date. (IFRS 13)

Fair value adjustment calculations

Goodwill is the difference between the cost of the acquisition and the acquirer's interest in the fair value of the identifiable assets and liabilities. So far we have used book value for the assets and liabilities. However, IFRS 3 states that we should use fair value. Therefore revaluations may be necessary to ensure that book value is equal to fair value.

Subsidiary

Revalues assets and liabilities to fair value

OR

Parent

Revalues assets and liabilities as a consolidation adjustment

Subsidiary's books unchanged

In the exam the usual scenario is that the subsidiary has not revalued to fair value and so a consolidation adjustment is needed.

23: The consolidated statement of profit or loss

Topic List

Consolidated statement of profit or loss

Consolidated statement of profit or loss and other comprehensive income

Under the revised IAS 1 the full statement is now called the 'statement of profit or loss and other comprehensive income'.

	Consolidated statement of profit or loss	Consolidated statement of profit or loss and other comprehensive income

Purpose	To show the results of the group for an accounting period as if it were a single entity
Sales revenue to profit after tax	100% P + 100% S (excluding dividend receivable from subsidiary and adjustments for intra-group transactions)
Reason	To show the results of the group which were controlled by the parent
Intra-group sales	Strip out intra-group activity from both sales revenue and cost of sales
Unrealised profit on intra-group sales	(a) Goods sold by P: increase cost of sales by unrealised profit
	(b) Goods sold by S: increase cost of sales by full amount of unrealised profit and decrease non-controlling interest by their share of unrealised profit
Depreciation	If the value of S's non-current assets have been subjected to a fair value uplift then any additional depreciation must be charged in the consolidated statement of profit or loss. The non-controlling interest will need to be adjusted for their share.

Transfer of non-current assets	Expenses must be increased by any profit on the transfer and reduced by any additional depreciation arising from the increased carrying value of the asset

The **net** unrealised profit (ie the total profit on the sale less cumulative 'excess' depreciation charges) should be eliminated from the carrying amount of the asset and from the profit of the company that made the profit.

For instance, H transfers an asset with a carrying value of $1,000 to S for $1,100. Depreciation is 10% p.a. The net unrealised profit is $90. This is debited to H's statement of profit or loss and to the carrying value of the asset.

Non-controlling interests	NCI% of S's PAT

Consolidated statement of profit or loss

Adjustments required

- Eliminate **intra group sales and purchases**
- Eliminate **unrealised profit** on intra group purchases still in inventory at the year end
- Eliminate **intra group dividends**
- Split profit for the year between group and NCI

Unrealised profit and losses:

Only where S sells to P, allocate the unrealised profit between NCI and P: *Debit* group retained earnings, *Debit* NCI, *Credit* inventory

Procedure

- **Combine all P and S results** from revenue to profit after tax. Time apportion where the acquisition is mid-year
- Exclude **intra group investment** income
- **Calculate NCI** (NCI% × PAT)

Consolidated statement of profit or loss and other comprehensive income

If there is a revaluation gain or loss in the parent or subsidiary you will prepare a consolidated statement of profit or loss and other comprehensive income. This will only require a few additions to the consolidated statement of profit or loss.

Revaluation gain in parent		Revaluation gain in subsidiary (80%)	
	$'000		$'000
Profit for the year	8,000*	Profit for the year	8,000*
Other comprehensive income:		Other comprehensive income:	
Gains on property revaluation	2,000	Gains on property revaluation	2,000
Total comprehensive income for the year	10,000	Total comprehensive income for the year	10,000
Total comprehensive income attributable to:		Total comprehensive income attributable to:	
Owners of the parent (5,000 + 2,000)	7,000	Owners of the parent (5,000 + (2,000 × 80%)	6,600
Non-controlling interest	3,000	Non-controlling interest (3,000 + (2,000 × 20%))	3,400
	10,000		10,000

*3,000 attributable to NCI

Notes

24: Accounting for associates

As you know, an investment can be carried at cost, fully consolidated or accounted for using the equity method, depending on the degree of control exercised. An associate is accounted for using the equity method.

Individual investor's books

- Carry at cost, or
- In accordance with IFRS 9 (at fair value)
- Using the equity method as described in IAS 28

Statement of financial position

Initial cost	X
Add/less: post acquisition share of profits/losses (before dividends)	X/(X)
Less: post-acquisition dividends received to avoid double counting	(X)
Carrying value	X

Consolidated financial statements

Use equity method unless:

- Investment acquired and held exclusively with a view to disposal soon
- Investor ceases to have significant influence

In these cases record at cost.

Statement of profit or loss

Group share of associate's PAT

25: Accounting for joint arrangements

Topic List

Joint arrangements

This area is most likely to come up in the groups question. The standards in this area have recently changed, so make sure you are familiar with their requirements.

IFRS 11 *Joint arrangements*

A joint arrangement requires **joint control**: the **contractually agreed** sharing of control over an economic activity.

```
                    ┌─────────────────────┐
                    │ Joint arrangements  │
                    └─────────────────────┘
              ┌──────────────┴──────────────┐
    ┌──────────────────┐          ┌──────────────────┐
    │  Joint ventures  │          │  Joint operations │
    └──────────────────┘          └──────────────────┘
```

Joint **ventures**	Joint **operations**
A joint arrangement whereby the parties that have joint control (the joint venturers) of the arrangement have **rights to the net assets** of the arrangement.	A joint arrangement whereby the parties that have joint control (the joint operators) have **rights to the assets, and obligations for the liabilities**, of that joint arrangement.

IFRS 11 states that where there is **no separate entity**, it is **always a joint operation**.

Accounting treatment (IFRS 11)

Joint venture

Use **equity method** in accordance with IAS 28

Joint operations

Recognise operator's interest in assets, liabilities, revenue and expenses

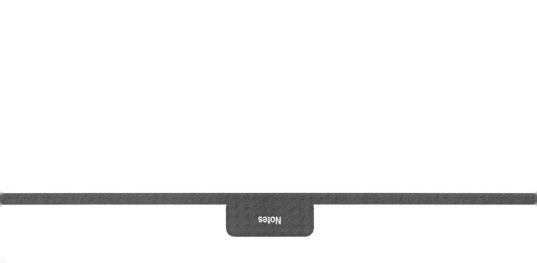
Notes

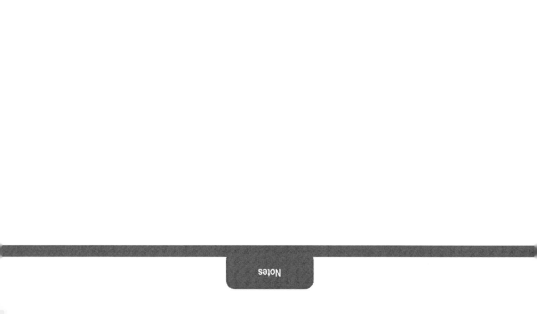
Notes

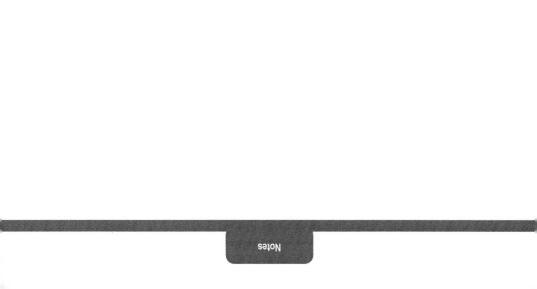

Notes

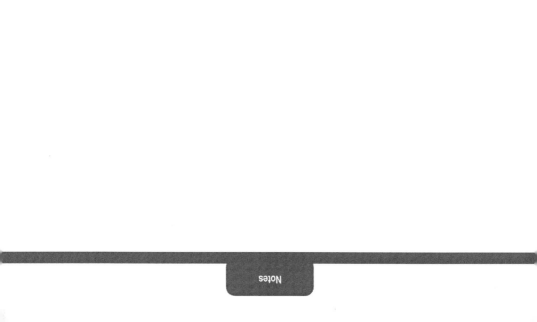

Notes

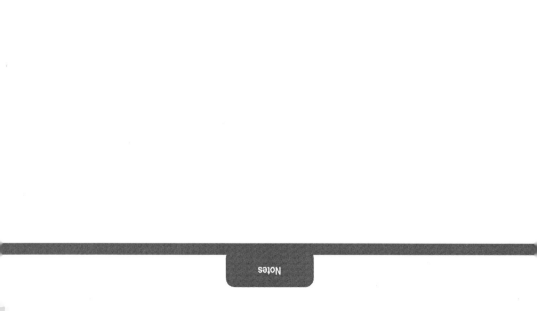

Notes